Mum,

A little bedtime reading
for you.

Enjoy!.

love,

Jane
xx

# HOMES & GARDENS

LIBRARY OF INTERIORS

Bathrooms

# HOMES & GARDENS
## LIBRARY OF INTERIORS

# Bathrooms

Vinny Lee

PAVILION

# To Sandy

First published in Great Britain in 1996 by
Pavilion Books Ltd
26 Upper Ground
London SE1 9PD

Copyright © Pavilion Books 1996
Photographs copyright see page 96
Designed by Peter Bennett
Picture research by Emily Hedges

The moral right of the publisher has been asserted.

A CIP catalogue record for this book is available from the British Library.

ISBN: 1 85793 784 8

Typeset in Gill Sans Medium
Printed and bound in Spain by Bookprint

10 9 8 7 6 5 4 3 2 1

This book may be ordered by post direct from the publisher.
Please contact the Marketing Department.
But try your bookshop first.

# Contents

# Introduction

The bathroom is one of the most intimate rooms in a house and the one in which people are most likely to indulge their imagination when it comes to decorating. A bathroom can also have dual uses – being both for the practical task of cleansing the body and a sanctuary in which to relax and unwind at the end of a long day.

These days bathrooms may also have a third purpose – either as a keep-fit area with an exercise bicycle, or as a dressing-room, if it is *ensuite* to a bedroom. With their increasing popularity, many home owners choose to transform a spare bedroom into an additional bathroom. With two bathrooms in the same house, one may be assigned to the children or guests and the other to the parents.

Showers are also growing more popular. A shower is a quick, invigorating way to start the day, as well as a refreshing cool-down after sport. Shower rooms represent the practical side of the bath regime and can be fitted

into small spaces, such as the area under a staircase or in a wardrobe recess in the bedroom. Showers are also economical on power and use far less water than baths, making them an ideal cost-saver in a family household.

The therapeutic pleasures and benefits of bathtime can be traced back to Roman times when, after bathing, slaves would dry, oil, and massage their masters' bodies. Nowadays aromatic bath oils and the gentle massage from jet sprays in showers and Jacuzzi fittings in a bathtub re-create a similar effect in the privacy of your own bathroom.

When it comes to planning and decorating your own bathroom, try to analyse the way you will use the room – whether you are a wash-and-go person or a stay-and-soaker, or whether you want a combination of the two. Lighting, flooring, fixtures and fittings can then be chosen both to create and enhance the desired mood and to provide the right facilities while making best use of the available space.

During the planning and preparation stage, do some thorough research. Look through magazines and brochures for inspiration, visit showrooms and DIY outlets to gauge prices and styles. At this stage it is wise to bear in mind the location of the main soil-pipe. As it is difficult and expensive to move this, it is advisable to ensure that your additional pipework will have easy access to it.

Draw a scale-plan of your bathroom and fittings. Cut out the lavatory, bath, separate shower (if you are having one), and hand-basin and arrange them on the room plan. Try several different versions until you reach the layout that suits you best. When you have your plan completed it is advisable to consult a qualified plumber.

A plumber's professional advice is invaluable when it comes to major installation work. He or she will also be able to keep you up to date with the newest fittings and developments, such as the macerator toilets that can be used in areas further away from the main soil-pipe because of the breakdown mechanism that is built into the system. Electrical work is best done by a professional, as there are many safety regulations that should be followed.

Once the plumbing, wiring and arrangement of the bathroom have been agreed, it is time to turn your mind to

the decoration of the room. Start with the flooring, and again ask yourself what sort of bathroom it is to be. If it is

for children or teenagers, the floor covering should be of the type that will not be adversely affected by water, and

one that is easy to mop up after a boisterous bathtime. Shower rooms are also a good place to use water-resistant

floor coverings, such as ceramic tiles or linoleum.

For an adult's *ensuite* bathroom you might consider taking the same

flooring through from the bedroom, or using a floor covering that

will complement the colouring and style of the bedroom. In

the more luxurious and indulgent bathroom you might like to have a carpet, but look

for one suited to bathrooms, that will withstand the pressure of damp and steam, as well as

being easy to vacuum or brush clean.

Bathroom floors should not only be water-resistant but must also be comfortable underfoot – especially barefoot.

Ceramic tiles can be cold to the touch, so cotton or towelling mats in front of the hand-basin, by the lavatory and

the bath will provide a more comfortable place to stand, but make sure that these have anti-slip backing.

Wooden floors well sealed and varnished will be water-resistant and the sealing should prevent splinters. Cork

tiles must be well sealed, most being sold already treated with a PVC coating, but check

to make sure, as untreated tiles may swell and then shrink and break if they get wet.

The colour and design of the flooring will also contribute to the overall scheme of the

room, so think of it in conjunction with your plans for the rest of the room. It is not

advisable to mix styles – for example, a Victorian panelled bath will look odd if you combine it with high-tech

chrome lever taps; fine metal blinds will look out of place in a country-style floral bathroom; and a bright, primary-

coloured, geometric tiled floor will be unsuitable for a pastel-coloured, traditional bathroom.

# Contemporary

Contemporary style can be divided into two areas – modern and ultra-modern. Modern bathrooms have the new shapes of bath, shower cabinet, toilet, basin and vanitory units in rooms that are decorated with clean and uncluttered style. The modern bathroom is sometimes an all-white affair, while others may have a wash of colour, such as ice blue, pale yellow or the zesty shades of orange, lime green and citrus yellow.

The ultra-modern bathroom is usually architect-designed and may feature a custom-made bath and units with the latest in chrome or steel fittings. Inspiration for this type of bathroom often comes from an industrial or Eastern source, with lever taps like those used in science or medical laboratories, and small tile mosaic walls and floors that are reminiscent of a Turkish steam-room.

The surroundings in which the ultra-modern, high-tech bath fittings are installed are often minimally decorated in monotone colours. But between these two contemporary approaches to bathroom design and the traditional style are a thousand blends and permutations.

Both the modern and ultra-modern bathroom may be required to change mood, from the efficient cleansing module that is needed for a quick start to the day to a restful haven of tranquillity at the end of a busy day. This mood change can be created in a number of ways.

Well-placed light fittings that can be controlled by a dimmer switch will allow the change from bright and active to soft and dusk-like, just at the twist of a button. The dimming of the light will also affect the colour of the walls

# Bathrooms

and fabrics that have been used in the bathroom to create a more soothing, restful atmosphere. In the evening or at a time of relaxation, a bath is essential for a long, luxurious soak. The cool, efficient colour scheme of the room, which is enhanced by bright morning light, can then be mellowed with low lighting that will darken and enrich the colours, making the room more intimate and cosy.

Even a subtle change, such as different towels, will enhance the feeling of relaxation. Soft, deep-pile towelling bathsheets will make drying more sensual and leisurely than a quick, brisk rub down with a waffle-weave cotton towel.

The bath, which may act just as an over-sized shower tray in the morning, can be transformed into a place for massage and water therapy at the touch of a control button that activates spa and Jacuzzi fitments. If you want to achieve the water-bubbling effect, but do not want to replace your bath, there are mats made of fine tubular plastic piping that can be placed in the bottom of the bath and will, when activated, achieve a similar effect to the built-in spa fitment.

When planning a bathroom for maximum efficiency allow adequate space to move and dry with ease. If the bathroom is to be used, for example, by a working couple who need to leave the house at the same time, make sure that there is ample room for two people to use the room simultaneously – space for them to pass, and for one to stand and dry while the other uses the hand-basin.

An ideal bathroom for such a couple would have a hand-basin each, so that there is no delay in access for brushing teeth, and so on. A shower is quicker and more invigorating in the morning than a bath, so a shower would be preferable in the interests of speed and space-saving.

Contemporary bathrooms owe much of their new style to the advances in materials from which baths and basins

are currently made. Acrylic baths now come in a comprehensive array of shapes and sizes, with variations such as

corner baths and baths with arm- and head-rests.

Acrylic also has the advantage of being warm to the touch, keeping the bath water

warmer for longer and being easy to clean. But the surface is less durable,

and when it comes to cleaning an acrylic bath or shower tray, it is

advisable to use a cream cleanser and a soft cloth because a

gritty or abrasive cleaner or cloth can scratch the surface.

Technology has also played its role in increasing the efficiency of the bathroom.

Temperature and timing controls can programme a shower or bath to turn itself on at a given time,

with water at a pre-set temperature.

The rise of the fitted bathroom has meant that a uniform finish can be achieved and maximum storage and closet

space provided. Many of the leading fitted kitchen companies and designers have turned their talents to bathroom

design, transferring the expertise gained in working around dishwashers and fridges to a room cluttered with hand-

basin, bath and shower unit. Specially tailored units and cabinets can be helpful in gaining

extra space in smaller or awkward-shaped bathrooms.

Modern bath shapes and fittings can look striking in plain, almost austere surroundings,

but they also suit some of the more fantastical ethnically inspired schemes, such as Aztec

or African. With these extravagant decorative themes it is important to bear in mind both safety and durability.

If the walls are to be painted to resemble those of a mud hut or an Inca temple, seal the finished paint effect to

protect it from the onslaught of water, steam and regular cleaning. And be wary when choosing decorative accessories, making sure that they do not have any dangerous fittings, such as sharp, obtruding metal edges or unsafe electrical wiring.

In the modern bathroom practical objects such as radiators can also be decorative. A number of radiator companies now make unusually shaped and coloured varieties and these, as well having a useful function, can be the

focal point of the room. The ladder radiator is also space-saving, as its narrow frame can be fixed high on the wall where it not only heats the room but dries wet towels.

Splashbacks behind hand-basins and baths can also be made from materials other than the more conventional perspex or ceramic tile. Sheets of fine steel can be cut into imaginative shapes and polished to produce smooth edges. The steel can be lacquered or varnished to prevent rust forming in damp and steamy bathroom conditions.

Contemporary bathrooms make ample use of metals such as steel and chrome, as well as reinforced glass fittings.

These reflective and transparent surfaces can be used to create a spacious feel and the design of many

of the fittings is minimal, adding to the uncluttered look.

Clinical trolleys, magnifying mirrors on expanding zigzag wall brackets, industrial chrome wastebins and single-support mirror and shelf units leave little doubt that the bathroom is the place for business, but under the light of a low-voltage bulb the modern bathroom can still have a relaxing charm. Creating a contemporary-style bathroom need not be inordinately expensive: the architect and designer look can be mimicked using standard units and carefully selected accessories from branches of stores such as Ikea, Texas, Bhs, Habitat and Homebase. For example, an inexpensive plain white or wood cupboard can be lifted with the addition of modern chrome or steel handles. Taking a fussy frame off a mirror, and fixing the mirror to the wall with capped screws, will create a chic and minimal appearance.

**B**elow: The clean, streamlined design of this uncluttered bathroom makes it an ideal room in which to carry out a quick morning cleansing routine. But, by dimming the recessed ceiling lights, you can create a warmer and more relaxing venue in which to take a leisurely bath. The small mosaic-style tiles used on the floor and walls not only provide an easy to clean, waterproof surrounding but also pattern in this one-coloured room.

In a plainly decorated bathroom accessories become an important feature. Chrome is a popular finish for contemporary items such as toothmugs, mirrors, towel rails and handles. Above left: The focal point of this grey tiled bathroom is a single-stem system with mirror, rail and shelf unit, which is both space-saving and functional. Above: This toothbrush-holder is an eye-catching feature on a shelf or basin surround. Chrome may be marked by water, but polishing with a soft cloth will remove marks.

**T**his simple bathroom, designed by architect Ed
Howell, has plain white tiles but avoids looking clinical
by the addition of bands of grey/blue trim. Ed has used
painted wood strips to divide the shower area from the
bath and to section off the large expanse of white wall.
All the woodwork in the room, such as the window
frames and skirting board, has been painted in the same
shade of blue. Shutters and an old-fashioned radiator
complete the rather geometric look.

**A** wall of mirrored doors conceals full-length cupboards in this spacious bathroom. The mirrors also reflect light and give a feeling of added space. The curved tiled wall, built to one side of the bath, provides a screen for a steel lavatory and basin, as well as an area for shampoo, taps and shower spray. Above right: Tall windows allow plenty of light to enhance the reflective surfaces, while austere white window shutters and a plain polished wood floor are in keeping with the design.

**H**aving two hand-basins and mirrors in a bathroom can speed up the morning teeth-cleaning and washing for a busy working couple – no more squabbling over who gets to use the basin first. This design is ideal for families with one bathroom on rushed school mornings, too. Although the shape of these basins would be suitable for an Art Deco-style bathroom, they have been given a contemporary setting here, with simple white tile surrounds.

**A**bove left: Fitted furniture has made its way from the kitchen to the bathroom. This custom-made unit with inlaid wood includes a large marble surround for the hand-basin as well as shelves and cupboards for clothes and towels. Above right: The wall of fitted cupboards in this simple, sunny yellow bathroom not only provides storage but the door in the foreground conceals the shower. When the doors are all closed the room has a neat and uniform appearance.

This ethnic scheme combines roughly painted sandy walls with Fired Earth's 'Multi-Coloured Slate' diamond-sawn floor tiles. Colour and pattern are introduced in vibrant towels and a kelim wall-hanging. Black taps, fittings and towel rails are more suitable in this scheme than the usual white or chrome versions. Right: Leading French designer Philippe Starck created this modern, but comfortably rounded suite for the maker Duravit. Its clean lines are suitable for most styles of bathrooms.

**A**bove left: Vola's 'America's Cup' stainless-steel basin and pedestal with etched, tempered glass surround and co-ordinating cabinet are eye-catching examples of modern design. With units that make such an impact, the main décor of the room can be kept plain. Above right: Sara May of Maya Design has used glass bricks to obscure the view but still allow light into the room. She has also  chosen bright vases and bottles to add colour to the plain white surroundings.

The distinctive rounded shape of this 'Richmond' sanitary ware from AquaWare would suit both modern and traditional-style bathrooms, but here it is in a setting that has an ethnic feel with rich green walls, dark wood window frames and a simple varnished brick floor. Strong colours on the walls will make a small room appear smaller, but in a larger room it will create a more intimate environment. Rich colours also provide an excellent background on which to display collections of artefacts.

**T**his 'Cabria' suite by Ideal-Standard is in a setting that has classical, almost Roman style. The cream and blue scheme is complemented by a geometric tiled floor in matching colours. The small square motif from the floor has been used to create a stencilled border around the room. The touches of red in the border can be echoed in the accessories, such as towels. The angular effect of the room is softened by the decorative wrought-iron panels on the windows.

**B**elow: This 'Palazzo' suite by Sottini is in 'Candleglow' – an off-white shade that complements the warmth of its Tuscan-style setting. To create this relaxed look a free-standing table and chair with cushion have been added. The floor is covered with terracotta tiles – floors like this should be sealed or treated to ensure that they will not be marked by water. Right: This single-lever mixer was designed by Philippe Starck for a range by Duravit. Its clean classic lines will suit most modern bathrooms.

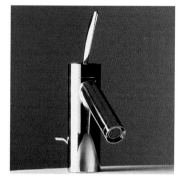

**T**hese vibrant red walls make an impact in the morning by daylight, but at night, by dimming the lights, the red will grow richer, warmer and more relaxing. The open shelf unit breaks up the space of this large room, creating two small areas, one for showering and washing, the other for the toilet and bidet. The open shelves also allow light from the window to circulate throughout the whole room. The rounded lines of the Palazzo suite by Sottini complement the uncluttered contemporary scheme.

# Traditional Bat

Traditional bathrooms cover a number of old-fashioned styles and variations – from bathrooms that are virtually copies of those created in the original era of interest to those that blend the charms of the old-fashioned life and the romantic ideas of the rural idyll.

The inspiration for a traditional bathroom can come from adapting an existing bathroom, such as an original suite left in a 1950s house; from the purchase or acquisition of old-fashioned bathroom fittings; or simply from a love of, or empathy with, the look associated with a particular period in history.

These days antique bathroom fixtures are much sought-after and some are highly collectable. Original china washing sets of basin and jug (or ewer) on a stand, with a matching chamber pot, take pride of place in many antique shops. Decorative porcelain lavatories and rolltop baths, as well as original taps and shower fixtures, can be found in the yards of salvage merchants. Those in less-than-perfect condition can be polished up, restored and re-enamelled in specialist shops. But if you cannot get hold of the original item, there are many companies making excellent reproductions.

The timeless appeal of the classic bathroom, whether inspired by Edwardian, Victorian or Art Deco styles, is perennially popular. Such bathrooms are often more decadent than their modern counterparts, with lush brass or decorative chrome fittings, rich and deep-coloured decorations and a wealth of authentic accessories.

With original or antique fittings and fixtures it is worth consulting your plumber to see whether they will have to

# hrooms

be adapted to work with modern plumbing standards and pipe sizes. The enamel finish on old baths may be chipped or damaged, but there are enamel repair kits and specialists available to restore the blemishes.

If you are planning to plumb in a cast-iron bath do check that the floor of the bathroom and the ceiling of the room underneath can take the weight – not only that of the bath itself, but also that of the bath when filled with water. Before you buy the bath it is worth taking time and a tape-measure to calculate how you are going to get the bath in place, especially if you have a narrow flight of stairs, tight access and a small bathroom door.

Other traditional bathroom features include a toilet with high-level cistern, which is wall-mounted above the toilet pan and flushed by a chain and pull. The old 'Thunderbox' was a toilet boxed with wood panels and a solid wooden bench, with a hole cut in the centre, placed across the top. The comfort of a wooden toilet seat is still sought after today, and looks the part in a traditional bathroom setting.

Victorian 'telephone' mixer taps with ceramic tops, or chrome Art Deco versions, will also help achieve an authentic look. Ceramic tiles with reproduction motifs are available in DIY shops and from tile merchants. For Art Deco style, try a simple checkerboard effect of black-and-white tiles. Where claw-foot baths stand proudly alone, showing off the fine curved lines and delicate feet of their design, other baths require the camouflage help of side panels. In a bathroom that features wood, perhaps in the skirting boards, under-basin cabinets and

cupboards, bath panels can be made of the same timber. The panels can be fixed in place either with sunken screws

that are filled to blend with the wood or with brass screws, caps and rings that become a feature of the panel. If

wood is used in a bathroom environment it should be oiled or varnished to make it water-resistant and to prevent

it warping in the steamy conditions.

Bath panels made from wood such as mahogany could be expensive, but a similar

effect can be achieved using a fake panel. The panel can be made from

plain MDF or plywood and then painted in a *trompe-l'oeil* style to

look like a piece of well-grained wood.

Such 'fake' effects can also be painted to resemble marble, granite or a whole range

of woods. Decorative beading can be added to the flat panel to give added interest to the

surface. If you do not want to add wooden beading you could try faking the effect with paints and a

brush, if you have artistic talents.

Wooden panelling can be used instead of ceramic tiles. In country-style bathrooms tongue-and-groove boards

are popular. These can be painted to match the chosen colour scheme. In a more stylized bathroom, panels may be

painted in rich colours, such as a red lacquer shade, and then stencilled with gilded designs and motifs.

The finishing touches to traditional bathrooms are important to create the authentic

feel. Light fittings should be in keeping with the period of the rest of the decoration.

Table lamps with Art Deco figurines or decorative Tiffany lights with their coloured glass

designs will create an interesting effect, or wall-mounted brass brackets with opaque

flame-shaped shades will add a touch of grandeur and Gothic style.

As with the main fittings such as bath and hand-basin, if you cannot find originals, or they are too expensive,

there are many good reproduction light fittings available. Some contemporary lighting devices, such as recessed ceiling spotlights, are so small and unobtrusive that they can be used without creating a clash of period styles.

Wooden and ceramic pull-handles for light fittings will make sure the room is correctly decorated down to the last

detail, but it is important to remember that panel light switches must not be used in a bathroom and may only be

placed on the outside or corridor wall adjacent to the bathroom, for safety reasons.

Traditional bathroom floors are often wooden or marble. Real marble tiles are not

only costly but are also very heavy, but you can create a similar effect using marble-effect

linoleum or tiles. For the Art Deco period, black-and-white tiles can be effective;

alternatively, if you do not wish to replace your flooring, a painted black-and-white

checkerboard effect can be reproduced on a plain wooden floor.

Victorian, Edwardian and country-style bathrooms are all complemented by wooden floors, which can be

polished, varnished or painted to suit the scheme. The inclusion of Persian rugs, carpet mats or rag rugs will add

comfort underfoot and will also add to the effect.

Decorative accessories and collections can be a real feature of period or country-style

bathrooms. Include ample shelving in your bathroom design, and old shaving equipment,

such as china shaving mugs and mirrors, collections of antique brushes, combs and

perfume bottles can all be arranged and displayed.

Ladies' travelling cases, pictures, books and even china plates can be put on walls and shelves to give a

lived-in and comfortable atmosphere to a bathroom. Old hat boxes, linen bags and baskets will not only look

attractive but can be used to provide invaluable storage space.

Traditional bathrooms take their inspiration from the past but use the best of modern

manufacturing techniques and up-to-date plumbing standards – to provide a bathroom

that can boast the best of both worlds.

**B**lue and white is a perennially popular colour scheme for bathrooms. In this country-style bathroom tongue-and-groove panelling has been used extensively, both at the side of the bath and as panelling along the walls. The white woodwork also complements the door which opens into the room. Tongue-and-groove can disguise uneven and cracked walls and provide extra insulation for a bathroom built against a cold, outside wall. The white paintwork and tiled border give a fresh appearance.

**T**op left: Although this room is traditional in style the flooring is modern and industrial. The heavy-duty rubber is waterproof and hard-wearing, but its colour makes it work in the overall scheme. Above: The side of this bath has been decorated with an ornate plaster detail. Plaster remnants can be found at salvage yards or copies made in resin can be bought from DIY shops; or, if you are artistic, you can make one with plaster of Paris. Left: Blue glass and china accentuate this gentian-blue wall.

**B**elow: This grand bathroom has Victorian overtones and dark wooden panelling. The bath is boxed in, as though it were a small four-poster bed, and the toilet has been cased in wood to resemble an old thunderbox. Careful attention has been paid to details such as the decorative frame of the mirror, which echoes the panel around the top of the bath. Right: Chinese designs were popular at the turn of the century. The rich red lacquer of these walls has been gilded with delicate oriental designs.

**O**ld mirrors, such as Victorian hall or overmantel mirrors, can be revamped to suit a bathroom setting. This ornate mirror, with useful small shelves, has been painted white and set on a rich blue wall. Left: A celestial theme pervades this room – blue walls with gold stars create a background for a gilded window. Osborne & Little make star print wallpaper in many colours, but you could also create a constellation on a painted wall using a rubber-star stamp and gold paint from the English Stamp Company.

The round window that is such a feature in this bathroom has also provided the inspiration for a decorative motif on the side panel of the bath. A marble surround and splashback are an old-fashioned but useful way of creating a waterproof area around the bath. The wooden wash-stand, now accommodating the hand-basin, also houses a collection of toiletries. In a bathroom which is not overlooked it is not necessary to worry about curtains or blinds for the window.

**A**bove: A bath in the centre of a room creates a luxurious feeling of space. In this room the only pattern is on the soft pink printed wallpaper. The decorative style of the paper is emphasized by the lack of any other competing pattern. Folding wooden shutters offer privacy with style. Left: This Gothic-inspired setting has walls painted to look like blocks of sandstone. Candles provide a romantic light for a night-time bathe and framed prints are tied together with broad burgundy ribbon.

**O**ld oak beams create a panelled effect in this country-style bathroom. A small wall built behind the hand-basin forms a cosy enclosure for the bath but also provides an area on which to place a mirror. Simple blue-and-white patterned tiles and a hanging display of plates give the room a homely and comfortable appearance. Right: A collection of blue-and-white plates and platters brightens up this bathroom, and the theme is reflected in the mix of old ceramic tiles used on the wall around the bath.

**A**bove left: This classic claw-foot bath is plumbed into the middle of the room using an obsolete chimney-breast to conceal the pipes. Simple polished wood flooring and plain white walls create a timeless and chic environment. Above: Fashion designer Margaret Howell uses old linen bags to store sponges, face cloths and sundries in her bathroom. The peg rail, which runs along the whole wall, also provides hanging space for dressing-gowns and large bathsheets.

**T**op left: A bath side panel like this could be created from a piece of inexpensive chipboard or MDF, decorated with square and diamond features made from beading, then painted in eggshell blue and white. Above: This Romanesque room has walls of bare plaster, which have an interesting texture, but the plaster must be sealed with varnish or a PVA bonding agent to protect it from steam and water damage. Left: This modern version of an old-fashioned bath rack still has classic appeal.

**B**elow: A minimal approach to decoration can be pleasing in a bathroom, and uncluttered surfaces will also make it easier to keep the place clean – which is especially important in a plain white bathroom where grime and marks will show. Right: Tortoiseshell paint effects have been used to decorate the side of the bath and the cupboard door in this seaside-inspired scheme. The walls are painted to resemble clouds and real sea shells are lined up around the wooden bath surround.

**R**ight: The storage space beside this basin has been constructed from an old chest of drawers with shelves added on top, forming a dresser. The tiled surround also makes a waterproof area on which to put shampoo, soap and other items that are likely to be damp. Below: The large expanse of mirror on the wall makes the room seem more spacious by reflecting the light back. The shelf above the mirror is an ideal place to display knick-knacks and collections such as these toy sailing boats.

**A**bove: The natural tongue-and-groove wood used in this bathroom should be treated with wax or a varnish to protect it from water damage. The panelling extends beyond the surface of the wall and provides a useful shelf. Left. Lighting around this hand-basin is supplied by two extendable brass fittings. It is important to have good, and preferably adjustable, lighting around a mirror for shaving and applying make-up, and a soft artificial light will give the correct appearance for night-time make-up.

# Tots, Teens &

The young, elderly and disabled require special facilities in bathrooms. It is a place where

people are not only vulnerable but are also subject to many dangers, such

as slipping and scalding. The smooth ceramic surfaces of the

bathroom suite are also difficult to grab hold of, if a person

is unsteady on his or her feet. As well as overcoming these dangers, it is important

that the temperature of the bathroom is comfortable. When the body is warm after a balmy

bath or shower it is an unpleasant shock to step out into a cold room and try to rub yourself dry.

While a warm room helps the water to evaporate, a cold environment makes it more difficult to get thoroughly

dry, and the rapid change in body temperature can be dangerous to the very young and the frail.

Having the temperature in the bathroom at a comfortable level is important for those who may take longer to bathe

and are more likely to be susceptible to feeling cold. Radiators should be plumbed into the main heating system –

never take electric heaters into the bathroom. It is very dangerous to have loose electrical

wires and appliances near water, so if you need a power point for an electric razor or

toothbrush, have a socket installed specifically for the purpose by a qualified electrician.

If radiators, which may be hot, are at a low level – starting at skirting board height, for

example – and could be touched by bare skin, it is advisable to put a cover over them. Heated towel rails should

also be carefully positioned for the same reason.

Radiator covers can be made by boxing in around the sides and covering the front with a mesh or grid that will

# Special Needs

allow the warm air to circulate easily. Or, if there is room, place a blanket box or similar sturdy piece of furniture in front of the radiator to keep a distance between the bathroom user and the heat source.

Bathroom manufacturers, well aware of the hazards connected with the bathroom, have developed many easy-to-install gadgets that can help reduce the number of accidents. They have also designed and developed special suites that give easy access for those who are wheelchair-bound or have reduced mobility.

One of the simplest, but most effective, safety devices is a slip-resistant rubber mat. The suckers on the back of the mat secure it to the bottom of the bath. Once installed, it prevents aqua-planing and gives the user, both young and old, a firmer area on which to stand, if showering, or to sit, if bathing. The mat will also provide a firmer base from which to get in and out of the bath.

Grab-rails on either side of the bath are also easily fitted and give the bather extra leverage and stability when settling into and rising from the water. Such rails can also be fitted by the lavatory to provide the same assistance.

Some manufacturers have created shower units with a shelf seat built into the surround. This type of shower is ideal for someone who finds it difficult to stand. Bath shapes with low sides also make it easier for the less mobile to gain access to a bath.

Water temperature can be controlled by thermostatic valves. These devices will prevent the temperature from reaching either extreme – too hot or too cold. And, as well as being popular in the most modern of bathrooms, lever taps are an excellent alternative to the traditional

turn tap, and much easier for arthritic hands.

For those who rely on a wheelchair or walking support, it is important to allow enough space in the bathroom

for the chair or walking aid to be turned and manoeuvred. A bell or call button in the bathroom will allow an

elderly or infirm person, who may require assistance, to have privacy to use the

bathroom alone but the ability to call for help when it is needed.

Children's bathrooms need to observe all the safety factors, but

they can also be a great place in which to indulge in a

decorating fantasy. A themed bathroom based on a cartoon, a comic-book hero, a

popular children's film or a nursery rhyme, can be tailored to suit children of all ages.

Transfers and stencils can be used to create a border if free-hand painting is beyond your ability.

A bright, primary-coloured bathroom will add to the fun of bathtime, and for a toddler who might be reluctant

to be washed and powdered before bedtime, an interesting and entertaining bathroom could be the way to coax

him or her in. Bright accessories such as primary-coloured towels and toothbrushes will also add to the fun, but

make sure that beakers and soap-holders are made of unbreakable plastic rather than china or glass.

Bathrooms that are subject to frequent waves and splashes of water from boisterous

bathtimes should be designed for easy mopping and cleaning. A good, waterproof seal

between the splashback and the side of the bath will help to prevent water seeping down

to the floorboards below and causing damp or rot.

Bath toys – all those rubber ducks and boats – should be tidied away between sessions into compact storage

units. If you have cupboard space that is fine; otherwise, colourful plastic stacking crates can provide a good

alternative and will not be affected by any water or dampness remaining in the toys.

Other storage space in the bathroom will be needed to hold medicines and cleaning fluids. Any harmful products should be kept well out of reach, preferably in a cabinet fixed high up on the wall and with a lock or child-proof catch.

If the bathroom is used for bathing and changing a baby, then a changing table or a mat on top of a cabinet will make the job easier and less of a strain on the back. Shelf space for talcum powder, creams and wipes is best kept near the changing table and a good-sized waste-bin for used nappies, cotton buds, and so on should also be to hand.

Bathrooms for teenagers are a good way of relieving the pressure on the main bathroom, especially when they are at an age when they seem to live in the bathroom! A small space can be adapted to accommodate an under-sized bath, shower or just a hand-basin and lavatory.

Teenagers' bathrooms can be decorated in many ways, whether it's with a wall-to-wall poster of the favourite football hero or pop idol or filled with a collection of sea shells, driftwood or kit-built aeroplanes. Whatever the theme, do check for safety before embarking on the decoration.

45

For both teenagers and younger children, having their own drawings and paintings on their bathroom tiles might be the focal point of the room. There are a number of ways to fix a drawing to a tile, such as a coat of clear varnish or transparent enamel paint which will hold the pattern fast, make it water-resistant and durable.

Children may also enjoy adding simple stencils or transfers to walls and bath surrounds, and even plain curtains can also be decorated with a theme by painting a motif using colourfast dyes such as those made by Dylon.

All bathrooms should be governed by safety as well as by practical and decorative dictates, but for the very young, the elderly and the less able-bodied it is even more important to check that everything has been done to ensure that bathtime is not only enjoyable but safe as well.

**B**elow: The splashback panel behind this bath has been specially cut and painted, not only to provide a protective shield for the wall but also to create a bright and fun backdrop. The outline for the scene was marked out on MDF and then cut, painted and sealed. The sections of the panel were then screwed into place and the joins filled with a flexible sealer to create a watertight surround. Right: Children's drawings can be permanently fixed to a tile with varnish, or glazed and fired.

**A**bove left: This small bathroom is an ideal way of giving teenagers their own space and leaving the main bathroom free for the rest of the family. In this room the silver lavatory seat and zany towel add an unconventional touch. Above: In plain surroundings accessories can speak volumes. Primary-coloured bath towels can bring a bright touch to even the starkest room. Left: Putting bathtime toys into stacking boxes, or hanging them up in drawstring bags like this, will keep them tidy when not in use.

**O**ne of the ultimate luxuries for a teenage girl is to have her own special bathroom. This pretty red-and-white scheme combines a floral paper with fabric that has a similar, but smaller, motif. The ruffled pelmet above the window and generous curtain under the basin give a feminine, but not overpowering, appearance to the room. Attention to detail will help to enhance the overall scheme of any room, and keeping accessories within the colour scheme will help achieve a co-ordinated look.

**T**his 'Avalon' bath from Twyford has a small level platform at the end furthest from the taps. This recess is ideal for toddlers to sit on, as they make their way in and out of the water. The decoration in this room has been inspired by an underwater scene from a fairy tale or cartoon. The full-size mural is colourful and entertaining and makes bathtime a special treat for a young person. The main theme is extended in the colourful sea creatures shelved well out of arm's reach.

**A**bove left: Mira's 'Excel Thermostatic' mixer shower is specially designed to avoid extremes of water temperature, so preventing scalding. This decorative theme is based on a nursery rhyme, the words of which are painted along the wavy decoration at the top of the wall. Above: The 'Liberty' three-piece mixer from AquaWare is useful for those with arthritic or limited hand movement, as the lever action makes it easy to turn the taps on and off.

**A**bove left: This bathroom is specifically designed for a wheelchair-user. Key requirements include space to manoeuvre a wheelchair safely and adequate heating. Above: The basin of Twyfords' 'Avalon' suite can be adjusted to suit wheelchair-users, and the lack of a base means that a chair can be brought close to the edge. The low side of the bath gives easy access, and support rails can also be positioned on either side of the lavatory.

# Showers & Sm

If you have one main bathroom in a family home, and school-aged children and parents

all need access to it at the same time, it might be worth looking at ways of

relieving the congestion. Putting a hand-basin in a bedroom is

perhaps the least expensive way to enable toothbrushing,

face- and hand-washing to take place away from the principal bathroom.

Looking for space to install a separate shower could be worth while, but consult a plumber

about the type of shower fixture that will be suitable for you. In an awkward space, where a

standard enclosed shower cabinet will not fit, it may be possible to create a waterproof environment by sealing the

area with PVA bonding and then tiling the walls, floor and ceiling. If you do opt to line an area wholly with tiles, do

check that the walls and floor are movement-free and can withstand the weight.

Shower rooms can be fitted into unused spaces, such as the sloping under-stairs area, an empty wardrobe

compartment or a boxroom. Showers are not only a quick and efficient way to wash,

but are also cost-effective and environmentally friendly, because the average shower

requires less water and power than a bath.

There are a number of different types of shower. Electric showers are connected to

the cold-water mains and the water is heated as required. The shower does not need to be attached to a roof-

height cold-water tank – as a pump can create sufficient pressure for a satisfying shower – or have access to the

hot water system, because the water is heated as it is pumped through the shower.

# all Bathrooms

This type of shower is economic and easy to install because of its independent heating mechanism, but it may be slower in cold weather because it takes longer for the water to heat up. Mixer showers draw water from the main household supplies. A mixer shower needs a height difference of at least 3ft 3in (1m) between the shower and the water tank. If the flow is sluggish you can add a power booster to increase the water's strength.

Power-showers are pump-assisted mixer showers with water supplies drawn from the main. These showers often have adjustable heads, which give different types of spray from hard and fine to heavy and soft – defined as massage, needle and champagne flows.

If you live in a hard-water area, a self-clean shower head is worth investing in. The self-clean head prevents the build-up of lime scale, which would, if it were allowed to accumulate, reduce the force and amount of water flow. Although the majority of showers have a single head, body jets can be wall-mounted and angled to give several sources of water spray. If you install jets, do ensure that the shower enclosure has a good waterproof seal and that the water tank can accommodate the extra water requirement.

As well as adjusting the flow of water, many showers can be used at a variety of heights. The shower heads can be clipped into a wall fitting or moved up and down a rail, from standard shower height to tap-level, or they can be hand-held for washing children.

A shower can also be installed over a bath, which saves space and negates the need for a

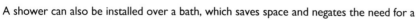

shower tray. But a shower curtain or hinged panel will be needed to prevent the floor from becoming waterlogged.

Shower curtains are prone to remaining damp after use and can develop fungus or mould growths. Keeping the

curtain clean by regular washing will help reduce the risk of mould, and leaving it pulled across the bath will give it a

better chance of drying thoroughly than if it is pulled back and left in tight furls.

Plain, unglamorous, plastic shower curtains can be disguised behind an outer curtain of

decorative fabric chosen to match or complement the other curtains or

blinds in the room. Reinforced glass panel doors can also be used in

conjunction with a bath shower. They are easier to clean,

and dry quickly, meaning they are less likely to grow mould.

Many free-standing showers are designed in their own prefabricated capsule, complete with

tray and shelves. These units come in a number of shapes, such as square and tubular, and usually

offer the most watertight accommodation for a shower.

In a shower room or small bathroom ventilation is very important. In the limited area available steam and

moisture will build up quickly and the moisture will linger in the air for some time after the bathroom has been

used. Good ventilation – whether a wall fan or one set into a window – will reduce the likelihood of fungal growths

on curtains and tile grouting.

When planning a small bathroom, take inspiration from other small dwellings, such as

yachts, houseboats and even aircraft, where compact living and economical use of space

are part of everyday life. If you follow a nautical theme you might like to take it as far as

adding a round, porthole-like window or skylight.

To make the most of the limited space available try to find fixtures that will have dual uses, such as a heated

towel rail, which will heat the room, dry the towel and provide a place to hang it. A shower over a bath will combine two uses in one space. If the area around the hand-basin is limited, fix a cupboard with a mirrored door above it to hold toothpaste, brushes, soap and daily toiletries.

Look around for smaller suites. There are many mini hand-basins and reduced-length baths, including a sit-in bath that is about half the size of a normal one but is deeper and has a built-in seat. Wall-hung toilets are also

economical on space, the pan being fixed to the wall so that there is no pedestal base and the cistern being hidden behind the panelling, with only the flush handle visible.

Electrically powered macerator toilet units are also useful for small and second bathrooms. These toilets can dispose of waste through smaller pipes and can be fitted in areas away from the main waste outlet, but they are not advisable for use as the main or only toilet in a house.

When planning the layout of a small bathroom, streamline fixtures and fittings. Try to line them up along a wall so that you can keep a clear passageway, giving easy access to all the facilities.

When decorating a small bathroom, choose colours from the lighter and brighter end of the colour spectrum. Dark colours will make the room seem claustrophobic and appear even smaller than it is. A large mirror or a wall covered with mirrored glass can have the effect of making the room seem larger, glass being also easy to clean and unaffected by damp and steam. The use of thick glass blocks or tiles instead of a solid wall will also create a feeling of space and light but still preserve modesty for a bather. Small bathrooms are often in places that lack windows so daylight will never be available. In these small internal rooms the selection and location of lighting are doubly important, as it will be the only source of light and has to cater for both morning and night-time washing and make-up requirements.

A well-designed small bathroom can be as effective and useful as a large one, but careful planning and organization are the key to success.

**A** wet room is a space devoted to shower or steam, and one in which the walls, floor and ceiling may all be tiled to withstand the onslaught of water. This wet room has a series of steps like a traditional steam room, so that the bather can sit and enjoy the warm moisture. The steps also usefully keep shampoos, soaps and body scrubs to hand. The shower shown here is Mira's 'Advance Memory Control', which can be programmed to come on at a designated temperature and power setting.

In this grand and spacious bathroom the shower has been installed in a deep recess. The surround of the edge of the shower enclosure has been framed with architrave to create a decorative archway, and the whole of the shower is lined with plain and pictorial blue Delft-style tiles. The design of the perfect shower is completed by choosing the right shower head. You may decide to plump for a constant volume of spray or invest in the luxury of an adjustable head.

**A**bove left: The shower in this ethnically inspired room is Mira's 'Realm' mixer shower with thermostatic control. The walls have been stippled to create a sand effect and even the pole supporting the tribal-print shower curtain has an appropriate decorative finish. Above: An extra wall has been built to make the third side of this shower cabinet – the new wall also provides an enclosure for the basin and mirror. The Romanesque style of this décor uses a warm pink marble and twisting mosaic border.

**T**his narrow passageway has been transformed into a Moorish shower room. The clever use of a white, keyhole-shaped archway leads the eye into the darker, tiled room with a curved floor and central drainage. A shower room like this does not restrict the bather as the confines of a cabinet or waterproof plastic curtain might, and allows for a large, centrally placed shower head, an impractical choice in many other showers. A ladder towel rail doubles as hanging space and heating.

This all-in-one 'Quadrant' shower enclosure by Ideal-Standard does away with the problems of leaks and seepage at the joins between walls, door and shower tray. This type of unit also makes maximum use of limited space – the angled back panels fit neatly into the corner of the room and the gently rounded front panel needs minimal room to open. The walls have been decorated with a harlequin-diamond pattern, which could be re-created using tiles set at an angle.

**A**djustable shower heads offer a variety of settings that can be changed to suit the type of shower you need or to suit your mood. Above left: Mira's '400' adjustable handset shows clearly how the settings vary. This 'Start' setting provides a wide-angle wetting spray. Left: This setting is referred to as 'aerated champagne' and gives a gentle, foaming spray, which is suited to a relaxing and unwinding wash. The '400' can be set on 'pulsating', recommended for using after sports.

**A**rmitage Shanks' 'Tribune Pentagon' angled enclosure offers good wide cabinet space in which to shower but uses space economically. This style of unit is useful in the corner of a bedroom or a small *ensuite* bathroom. Here tiles have been chosen to co-ordinate with the starry wallpaper. The mix of plain, star and crescent moon tiles creates an interesting background to the shower, a theme  echoed in the crescent moon and other accessories displayed on the small table.

In a loft conversion or attic space it is not always possible to have clear standing height in the whole area. When planning a bathroom with this sort of restriction, think through your movements in the bathroom. For example, if you are sitting upright in the bath, the end at which your feet are can be in an area of restricted height, as long as there is enough space to sit comfortably at the other end. In the room pictured, a bath under the eaves makes the most of the available space.

**R**ight: The cistern of this lavatory has been boxed in and shelves have been added above to create a dresser. This clever use of the 'dead' space around a lavatory provides added display areas and a pleasing finish in a small bathroom. Below: If you have a room that would be cramped with a three- or four-piece bathroom suite, think about putting the hand-basin in the bedroom and the bath and lavatory in another room, or the lavatory and basin in one room and the bath in the bedroom.

**F**itted units along one wall and wall-mounted ladder towel rails on either side of the window take up a minimal amount of space in this small bathroom. This careful planning has left enough room for an elegant, central bath. Folding doors are also space-effective, since they double back on themselves rather than requiring full door width to open and close. When space is tight it is useful to know that baths come in a variety of sizes, so do not be put off by average-size fittings.

When planning a small, narrow bathroom like this it is best to keep the units that will be used most, such as the toilet and hand-basin, nearest the door. The bath, which might be used only once a day, can be positioned further away. A corner hand-basin could be used in an awkward space, and industrial sinks with narrow bowls can be used in the appropriate domestic setting. A linear plan gives easy central access to each unit and creates a feeling of depth, while pale walls, suite and tiling reflect light.

**A**bove: The 'Studio' range by Ideal-Standard has been specifically designed for small bathrooms. The semi-countertop, wall-mounted basin can be set into the top of a cupboard or have a unit built beneath it to give extra storage space. The rounded lines of the suite also make it easier to move around. Here, tongue-and-groove panelling has been used to hide the cistern, while providing a shelf to hold toiletries. A system of decorative stacking boxes is both attractive and space-efficient.

**A**nother suite specifically designed for small rooms is Twyfords' 'Galerie'. The wall-mounted basin takes up the minimum of floor space and the lavatory cistern is behind the panelling. Two large metal bins have been sunk into the panelling at an angle, providing unusual but useful storage. Their diamond shape is echoed in the towel-hanger above the bath and in the mirror above the basin. A lace curtain has been hung over a dull plastic shower curtain to create a more elegant effect.

**A** false wall has been built to create a third side to this tiled shower enclosure, which uses two existing walls for the other sides. As the floor is also terracotta-tiled and the accessories in the bathroom are minimal, steam and dampness from the shower are not a problem, so no door or curtain has been added to fill the fourth side. The hand-basin has been plumbed into an ornate metal washstand, and the bright yellow ceramic bowl adds to the primary colour scheme of the room.

In confined spaces soft, fabric curtains offer a better option than hard, angled wooden cupboards. The curtain provides a screen for shelves filled with spare toilet rolls and can enhance the overall décor of the room. Pulling back a curtain also requires less space than opening a wooden door, and if your elbows jut out over the edge of the bath when bathing you will find it more comfortable to touch the folds of a curtain than the bruising solidness of a cupboard panel.

## 7

**A**bove: This stylish linear bathroom has a stained-glass window, which draws the eye to the end of the room, creating an impression of length. The window is decorative enough to obscure the view but still allows the light to come in. A small dividing wall at the end of the bath creates smaller units within the main area, which also adds to the feeling of space. Left: The red borders below the ceiling, above the tiles and skirting enhance the feeling of height in the room.

The compact 'Carousel' suite by Shires offers a full bathroom suite but on a smaller scale, which is an ideal solution for a second, *ensuite* or spare bathroom. In this scheme the rustic appearance is enhanced by the exposed beams and the rough brick wall. To prevent shaling the bricks should be painted with a solution of PVA or a bonding material, which will make the surface water-resistant and durable. The wooden beams are complemented by wooden shutters at the windows.

**C**orner baths are useful in small rooms because they can be plumbed into awkward spaces. This 'Firenze' suite from Shires' 'Visions' range fits neatly into the corner and leaves ample space for the lavatory and hand-basin. Louvre shutters add to the crisp, uncluttered look of this room and are a good alternative to curtains when so close to a bath. Painted shutters are resistant to water and fit neatly into the window frames, whereas fabric curtains may become damp, mouldy or damaged.

**V**arying levels in a small bathroom can also create a feeling of space. The toilet in this room has been raised up by two steps to set it above and back from the main floor area. The glass brick wall makes the room lighter and less claustrophobic than a solid wall might. The 'Polka Naiad' corner bath from Shires has a rounded front, which gives easy access to the hand-basin in this compact setting. The design also allows for shelves around the bath and behind the hand-basin.

**A** feeling of depth is created in this room by the use of narrow floorboards radiating out from the corner where the bath is. If the boards had been laid in straight lines parallel to the bath the floor would have the appearance of being narrower, whereas this design gives the impression that the bath is in a distant corner rather than close by. The 'Martinique' offset corner bath by Shires is classically simple and understated, so it does not overpower in a small room.

# Dual-Purpose

Many bathrooms are now used for more than just morning and evening ablutions.

Bathrooms are favoured places in which to rest and relax as well as to

exercise and keep fit. Some bathrooms double as greenhouses and

are used to display and grow tropical plants, and with a

ready supply of water to hand some even double as laundry rooms.

Bedrooms with *ensuite* bathrooms are increasingly popular. The luxury of being able to step

from the privacy of one room to the other is an indulgence many people now enjoy. Linking the two

rooms can provide extra space, which may be used for a related purpose.

The area between bed- and bathroom is ideal for a dressing-room, wardrobe and storage area, or boudoir in

which to dress and undress, or just relax. But bathrooms that double as dressing-rooms, or are part of a bedroom

where clothes are stored, should be well ventilated to prevent clothes becoming damp and musty.

Turning a small spare bedroom into an extra bathroom often provides the kind of

room that gives enough space for activities other than bathing. With the addition of a

*chaise-longue* or an upholstered armchair and a stack of books or magazines, such a

room can become a study or den. To create a room within a room or to shield an area,

a screen or group of screens can be used to make a movable wall.

Bathrooms with large areas of wall space can be transformed into a picture gallery with paintings or family

photographs. Displays of collections such as china, fans or other artefacts can also provide an interesting feature.

# Bathrooms

Some bathrooms that have been created from spare bedrooms retain the old fireplace.

This central feature to the room can be re-kindled by the addition of a gas log fire, which is

not only decorative and adds extra heat but can bring a romantic atmosphere to the room.

On a more practical note, when plumbing arrangements for a bath, lavatory and hand-basin

are already in place it is easy enough to add extra facilities, such as a washing machine. If, as is often the case, the

laundry basket is already in the bathroom, then it is only a short distance to take the dirty clothes to the machine.

Retractable washing lines can be fixed above the bath to provide extra drying space for clothes. As pipes, heating

and hot-water tanks tend to make the bathroom one of the warmer rooms in the house it is an ideal

place to dry clothes.

With the current interest in keeping fit a large bathroom with plenty of floor space is an

ideal place to keep equipment such as rowing or cycling machines. The floor area can

also be used to do sit-ups and other exercises. After building up a sweat from strenuous activity

it is ideal to be able to strip off and step straight into the shower, therapeutic whirlpool or spa bath.

The greenhouse bathroom appears in many guises, from a few pot plants dotted around shelves and the tops of

cupboards to an abundance of vegetation squeezed into every possible space. The

warmth and moisture of the bathroom suit many types of plant, but do check the

favoured conditions on the plant's label before buying.

Plants can be decorative, but some scented varieties can also add to the enjoyment of a long leisurely soak by filling the warm, moist air with their perfume. Bathrooms are sometimes windowless and

therefore lacking the sunlight that most plants need, so if your favourite plant begins to look a little yellow around

the edges, take it outside for a few weeks to recover and replace it temporarily with another.

Lemon geraniums and herbs such as sage, thyme and marjoram are both scented and attractive, and they enjoy

the environment of a bathroom. Certain orchids thrive in the humidity but do need

access to daylight.

Glossy-leaved plants, such as the Kangaroo Vine (*Cissus*

*antarctica*) and the Castor-Oil Plant (*Fatsia*), will thrive in

cooler bathrooms. The Sweetheart Plant (*Philodendron scandens*), with its decorative

heart-shaped leaves, is another useful plant, and in the United States it is actually known as

the Bathroom Plant because it grows so well in that room. *Anthurium* are not easy to grow but, once

settled, their shiny red 'Painter's palette' flowers are a spectacular sight.

The decorative-leaved *Calathea* and *Manranta* (Prayer Plant, Herringbone Plant, Peacock Plant, Zebra and

Rattlesnake Plants) do not like direct sunlight, so in dark or windowless bathrooms these plants will be happy, and

they will do best in a warm room with a constant temperature. Ferns, such as the Sword, Boston, Feather and Lace

varieties, like warmth, light and humidity.

All plants kept in the bathroom should be sprayed regularly – so give them a rinse with

the shower attachment to wash off dust and any powder or spray residue that may have

settled.

Pot plants can be attractively displayed in china cache-pots or decorative containers, such as old china teapots,

bowls, cups and jugs, or in standard terracotta planters that have been painted with waterfast colours.

Plants may thrive in a well-heated bathroom, but it would take a tropical plant to cope with the conditions of a steam-room or a sauna. These facilities can be added to large bathrooms but will require extra insulation and building work to retain the heat that is generated within them.

The decoration of a dual-purpose bathroom should reflect both uses. For example, if the bathroom is also a boudoir where you rest and relax, then the floor may be carpeted and curtains are more likely to be of fabric, with a pelmet and possibly tie-backs, adding to the feeling of comfort.

If the bathroom is also a place for exercise and activity, the area may be tiled – both walls and floor – and the windows covered by a roller- or slat-blind, emphasizing the sense of industry and energy.

As the bathroom tends to be the most private room in the house, you can really indulge in your fantasies when it comes to choosing your furnishing style. Whatever second purpose you choose to add can be the basis for a decorative theme.

A study-cum-bathroom, for example, might be lined with bookshelves and, instead of a fabric-upholstered armchair, you could go for a leather-covered, gentlemen's club chair. If there is a fireplace, surround it with a club fender, and even a desk could be added, not just to keep papers in, but also to store towels, tissues and soaps. For the ultimate in decadence and seduction, fill the bathroom with candles and turn off the main lights. Bathing by candlelight is one of the most relaxing and seductive sensations and scented candles can make it even headier. When your bathroom is your personal, private chamber you can really push the theme to the limits.

As with all bathrooms, the dual-purpose bathroom should be carefully planned and organized. Safety is important and, in a room where you may need extra electrical power points for equipment such as a washing machine or for the digital display on a rowing machine, consult a professional electrician before installing additional sockets.

**A** large bedroom can be divided to provide separate bathing and sleeping areas. A large folding door, like the one seen here, can be closed to give privacy in either room or opened to give a through space. Full-length curtains would make good alternatives as room dividers. The ornate old hand-basin and style of bath have been chosen to complement the traditional-style bed and décor in the adjoining room. When a room is arranged in this way adequate ventilation is of primary importance.

*E*nsuite bathrooms sometimes double as exercise or dressing-rooms, and when rooms interconnect it is important that colours and patterns in the two rooms are sympathetic. The white and pale blue shades used in these two rooms blend well together. The plain wooden flooring also unites the two areas and, for warmth on getting out of the bed or bath, has been covered with a decorative rug in the bedroom and a cotton mat in the bathroom.

**R**ight: Some bathrooms double as greenhouses or
plant display areas. The damp, warm atmosphere of
bathrooms suits many types of tropical plant. Rich green
and variegated foliage can be very attractive on its own,
although the occasional bloom does add to the pleasure.
Below: Although the flowers in the pots on either side
of the bath are fake, they add a cottagey feel to the
room. A cabinet displaying decorative plates illustrated
with pictures of birds and flowers enhances the effect.

**T**op left: This small cloakroom has jungle fever; not only are there real plants with abundant foliage but the theme has been carried through in the choice of wall colour, printed paper panel and padded seat cover. Above: In this vivid green bathroom a row of geraniums and other plants breaks up a long expanse of wall. The plants are potted up in a variety of containers from terracotta plant pots to glazed green cache-pots. Most plants grow best if they have contact with sunlight.

The boxed-in area above this bath serves as a substitute mantelpiece with a clock and trinkets displayed upon it. An easy chair beside the bath adds to the feeling of a relaxed and intimate boudoir or study, as well as a practical bathroom. Framed pictures and a potted plant in a decorative basket enhance the feeling of leisurely repose. The ruched window blinds are a practical but attractive way of shielding a bather from view, but save the fabric from the direct line of damaging splashes.

**A**bove: With a roaring fire in the grate and a comfortable armchair beside it, this room is a peaceful sanctuary as well as a place in which to wash. It is a place to linger in – long, cosy conversations and perhaps a glass or two of wine would seem appropriate here. Top left: The *chaise-longue* indicates that there is no hurry to leave this bathroom either, and fitted wardrobes along one wall indicate that the room doubles as a dressing-room-cum-boudoir.

In this spacious room there is enough empty floor area to conduct a general keep-fit routine, but the easy basket chair and cane table with candle and books would seem to indicate a place of relaxation rather than exercise. The plain white and wood décor of the room is lifted by a finely patterned dhurrie on the floor and a printed ethnic throw draped back at the window. Clean lines and a mirrored wall behind the bath make an already adequate room seem even larger.

## 8

**A**bove: This gentleman's bathroom is part den. Keeping his ties hanging in the warm, sometimes steamy bathroom will help the wrinkles and folds drop out. As washing is invariably preceded or followed by dressing, having the two functions side by side saves time. Left: Small bedrooms may lack storage space for clothing, so a large bathroom can be a godsend. This linen press is ideally placed in the bathroom; clean clothes and bath towels can be stored where they are most often needed.

This bedroom is also a bathroom. The whole scheme has been devised to create a room that exudes luxury. The bath is curtained off in the same fabric used for the half-tester at the bed-head, and in this case, the cleansing and scrubbing side of bathing are overidden by its sensual and relaxing pleasures. Although it is rare to add a bed to a bathroom, it is not uncommon to put a bath into a large bedroom, although lavatory and hand-basin facilities are usually kept in a separate room.

**I**n dual-purpose bathrooms storage is important. Not only will there be the usual bath products and towels but also books, board games and exercise equipment, or whatever else is required. Fitted units can be used to incorporate hand-basins and utilize the space underneath. Here fitted units by Smallbone in both these bed- and bathrooms keep floor and surface areas tidy, hiding the clutter of shampoos and other items neatly under the hand-basin.

In a stark white bathroom designed by Michael Daly, a display of terracotta and black prints based on classical Greek myths, in toning red-and-black wood frames, transforms a plain bathroom into an inspiring gallery. The extendable shaving mirror and panels of mirror tiles allow reflection to multiply the prints to stunning effect. Framed prints and photographs should be well sealed to prevent damp from seeping under the glass and damaging the image.

**A**n antique washstand with ceramic bowl has been adapted and plumbed in to provide a wash-basin with traditional style. The rich terracotta walls give a strong backdrop on which to display a collection of black-and-white portraits and classic prints. The white panel below the terracotta picks up the white of the ceiling and the roll-top bath. Two old glass lampshades are grouped above the hand-basin and also cast a light over the large print underneath.

# Directory

## BATHS AND SUITES

**Armitage Shanks Ltd**, Armitage, Rugely, Staffs, WS15 4BT. Tel. 01543-490253.

**Aston Matthews**, 141–147a Essex Road, Islington, London, N1 2SN. Tel. 0171-226 7220. 25 models of cast-iron baths in 16 sizes.

**Bathroom City**, Amington Road, Tyseley, Birmingham, B25 8ET. Tel. 0121-708 0111. Also branches at Lowesmoor Wharf, near Shrubhill Station, Worcester. Tel. 01905-613649; Sir Matt Busby Way, Stretford, Manchester. Tel. 0161-877 1110; and 54 Call Lane, City Centre, Leeds. Tel. 01532-430492.

**Colourwash**, 165 Chamberlayne Road, Kensal Rise, London, NW10 3NU. Tel. 0181-459 8918. All new bathroom-ware, accessories and planning advice.

**Dorset Reclamation**, Bere Regis, near Poole, Dorset. Tel. 01929-472200. Fax 01929-472292.

**Doulton Bathroom Products**, Lawton Road, Alsager, Stoke on Trent, Staffs, ST7 2DF. Tel. 01270-884333.

**Drummond's of Bramley**, Birtley Farm, Horsham Road, Bramley, Guildford, Surrey. Tel. 01483-898766. Refurbished period bathrooms and fittings.

**C. P. Hart**, Newnham Terrace, Hercules Road, London, SE1 7DR. Tel. 0171-928 5866. Stockists of Duravit, AquaWare.

**Ideal-Standard Ltd and Sottini**, Bathroom Works, National Avenue, Kingston upon Hull, N. Humberside, HU5 4HS. Tel. 01482-346461. Fax 01482-445886.

**Max Pike Bathrooms**, 4 Eccleston Street, London, SW1W 9LN. Tel. 0171-730 7216.

**Original Bathrooms**, 143–145 Kew Road, Richmond, Surrey, TW9 2PN. Tel. 0181-940 7554.

**Pipe Dreams**, 70 Gloucester Road, London, SW7 4XX. Tel. 0171-225 3978.

**Shires Bathrooms**, Beckside Road, Bradford, W. Yorks, BD7 2JE. Tel. 01274-521199. Fax 01274-521583.

**Trent Bathrooms**, PO Box 209, Hanley, Stoke on Trent, Staffs, ST1 3RR. Tel. 01782-202334. Fax 01782-285474.

**Twyfords Bathrooms**, Lawton Road, Alsager, Stoke on Trent, Staffs, ST7 2DF. Tel. 01270-879777. Their 'Avalon' suite is featured in the Tots, Teens & Special Needs chapter on page 51.

**The Water Monopoly**, 16/18 Lonsdale Road, London, NW6 6RD. Tel. 0171-624 2636. Refurbished period baths.

## SHOWERS

**Aquadart**, 7 Wycliffe Industrial Park, Leicester Road, Lutterworth, Leicestershire, LE17 4HG. Tel. 01455-556561. Space-efficient shower cabinets and fittings.

**Aqualisa Products Ltd**, The Flyers Way, Westerham, Kent, TN16 1DE. Tel. 01959-563240. Fax 01959-564937.

**Armitage Shanks Ltd**, Armitage, Rugely, Staffs, WS15 4BT. Tel. 01543-490253. Shower enclosures such as Tribune Pentagon. For helpline and stockist details tel. 01454-322888.

**Caradon Mira Ltd**, Cromwell Road, Cheltenham, Glos, GS52 5EP. Tel. 01242-221221. Fax 01242-221925.

**Coram UK Ltd**, Scafell Road, Lytham St Anne's, Lancs, FY8 3HZ. Tel. 01253-728443. Range of shower enclosures.

**Hansgrohe**, Unit D2, Sandown Park Trading Estate, Royal Mills, Esher, Surrey, KT10 8BL. Tel. 01372-465665. High-quality contemporary bathroom equipment.

**Matki plc**, Freepost BS7214, Yate, Bristol, Avon, BS17 5BR. Fax 01454-315284. Shower surrounds and doors.

**Nordic**, Unit 5, Fairview Estate, Holland Road, Hurst Green, Oxted, Surrey, RH8 9BZ. Tel. 01883-716111.

**Trevi Showers**, PO Box 60, National Avenue, Kingston upon Hull, N. Humberside, HU5 4JE. Tel. 01482-470788. Fax 01482-445886.

**Triton plc**, Triton House, Newdegate Street, Nuneaton, Warwicks, CV11 4EU. Tel. 01203-344441.

## SPAS

**Hydraspa**, Unit 2, Crossgate Drive, Queen's Drive Industrial Estate, Nottingham, NG2 1LW. Tel. 01602-866444. Fax 01602-866440.

**Jacuzzi UK**, 17 Mount Street, London, W1Y 5RA. Tel. 0171-409 1776.

## TAPS

**C.P. Hart**, Newnham Terrace, Hercules Road, London, SE1 7DR. Tel. 0171-928 5866.

**Pegler Ltd**, St Catherine's Avenue, Doncaster, S. Yorks, DN4 8DF. Tel. 01302-368581.

## ACCESSORIES

**Aero**, 96 Westbourne Grove, London, W2 5RT. Tel. 0171-221 1950. Modern accessories, bath racks, soap trays, etc.

**The Bath House**, Liberty, 210–20 Regent Street, London, W1R 6AH. Tel. 0171-734 1234.

**Black Country Heritage**, Britannia House, Mill Street, Brierley Hill, West Midlands, DY5 2TH. Tel. 01384-480810 for brochure and nearest stockists.

**The Conran Shop**, Michelin House, 81 Fulham Road, London, SW3 6NR. Tel. 0171-589 7401.

**Descamps**, 197 Sloane Street, London, SW1X 9QX. For nearest outlet tel. 0171-235 6957. A wide range of both traditional and modern towels, bathrobes and bath accessories.

**Designer's Guild**, 277 King's Road, London, SW3 5EN. Tel. 0171-351 5775. Bright contemporary fabrics and accessories.

**English Stamp Company**, Sunnydown, Worth Matravers, Dorset, BH19 3JP. Tel. 01929-439117. Fax 01929-439150. Large selection of rubber stamps, including stars, fish, shells and starfish, also gold paint. For brochure and further details tel. as above.

**Global Village**, For nearest stockist tel. 01460-40194. Wide range of ethnic artefacts, candlesticks and furniture.

**Graham & Green**, 7 Elgin Crescent, London, W11 2JA. 0171-727 4594. Wide range of traditional and contemporary accessories.

**Habitat**, For nearest branch tel. 0171-255 2545. Wide range of contemporary and traditional-style accessories, bath products, dressing-gowns and towels.

**Heal's**, 196 Tottenham Court Road, London, W1P 9LD. Tel. 0171-636 1666.

**The Holding Company**, 243–245 King's Road, London, SW3 5EL. Tel. 0171-352 1600. Fax 0171-352 7495. Cupboards and small bathroom storage; many unusual ideas from America and Italy.

**Ikea**. Tel. 0181-451 5566 for nearest branch and catalogue. Flooring and storage systems.

**Keuco**, Ardenoak House, 101 High Street, Tring, Herts, HP23 4AB. Tel. 01442-890907. Fax 01442-890997. Cabinets and storage units.

**Muji**, 26 Great Marlborough Street, London, W1V 1HB. Tel. 0171-494 1197. Branches in London WC2 and Glasgow. Good storage, towels and bath products.

**W.H. Newson and Sons Ltd**, 491 Battersea Park Road, London, SW11 4LR. For brochure and other branches tel. 0171-223 4411. Architrave moulding to create panel details and decorative edging; also stockists of PVA and similar bonding agents, MDF, chipboard, plywood, etc.

**Osborne & Little**, 304 King's Road, London, SW3 5UH. Tel. 0171-352 1456. Star wallpapers in a variety of shades; also other papers, accessories, braids and trims.

**The Pier**, 91–95 King's Road, London, SW3 4PA. For details of ten other branches tel. 0171-351 7100. Many unusual bathroom accessories, bathmats, rugs in traditional, ethnic and contemporary styles.

**Purves & Purves**, 80–81 & 83 Tottenham Court Road, London, W1P 9HD. Tel. 0171-580 8223. Contemporary accessories.

**Stiffkey Bathrooms**, Stiffkey, Wells-Next-the-Sea, Norfolk, NR23 1AJ. Tel. 01328-830084. Unusual lights, lavatory-roll holders and fittings.

**Tom Tom**, 42 New Compton Street, London, WC2H 8DA. Tel. 0171-240 7909. Fifties, Sixties and Seventies lights, wastepaper baskets, storage systems and chairs.

### BATH RE-ENAMELLING

**Bath Re-enamelling Service**, Chapel Court, 70 Hospital Street, Nantwich, Cheshire, CW5 5RF. Tel. 01270-626554.

### FLOORING

**Amtico**, 18 Hanover Square, London, W1A 9EA. Tel. 0171-629 6258.

**Criterion Tiles**, 196 Wandsworth Bridge Road, London, SW6 2UF. Tel. 0171-736 9610.

**First Floor**, 174 Wandsworth Bridge Road, London, SW6 2UQ. Tel. 0171-736 1123. Industrial and heavy-duty floorings as well as linoleum and vinyl.

**Forbo-Nairn Ltd**, PO Box 1, Den Road, Kirkcaldy, Fife, KY1 2SB. Tel. 01592-643111.

**Harwood Flooring Co.**, 146–152 West End Lane, West Hampstead, London, NW6 1SD. Tel. 0171-328 8481.

**Inlaid Rubber Flooring Company**, 199 Marsh Road, Pinner, Middx, HA5 5NE. Tel. 0181-868 2462.

**Junckers**, Wheaton Court Commercial Centre, Wheaton Road, Witham, Essex, CM8 3UJ. Tel. 01376-516512. Specialist wood flooring company.

**Marley Floors Ltd**, Dickley Lane, Lenham, Maidstone, Kent, ME17 2DE. Tel. 01622-858887.

**Siesta Cork Tiles Ltd**, Dept 5/95, Unit 21, Tait Road, Croydon, Surrey, CR0 2DP. Tel. 0181-683 4055.

**Sinclair Till**, 793 Wandsworth Road, London, SW8 3JQ. Tel. 0171-720 0031. Decorative design and cutting service; stockists of vinyl and linoleum.

**Stone Age**, 19 Filmer Road, London, SW6 7BU. Tel. 0171-385 7954/5. Fax 0171-385 7956. Sandstone and limestone flooring.

### INTERIOR DESIGNERS AND ARCHITECTS –

work featured in this book

**Michael Daly**, interior designer. Tel. 0171-352 8623.

**Ed Howell**, of architects Carrick, Howell and Lawrence, can be contacted on 01372-844593.

**Sara May**, of Maya Designs, 80 Duke Street, London, W1M 5DQ. Tel. 0171-409 0902.

### LIGHTING

**Christopher Wray**, 600 King's Road, London, SW6 2DX. Tel. 0171-736 8434. Period-style and contemporary light fittings.

**John Cullen**, 585 King's Road, London, SW6 2EH. Tel. 0171-371 5400. Lighting advice and schemes, as well as the latest in contemporary lighting techniques and fittings.

**McCloud**, 269 Wandsworth Bridge Road, London, SW6 2TX. Tel. 0171-371 7151. Antiqued and classical-style wall brackets and lightings; also some pieces of furniture.

**Mr Light**, 279 King's Road, London, SW3 5EW. Tel. 0171-352 8398. Large range of contemporary lighting.

**Silvertown Hi-Tech Lighting**, Springwood Drive, Springwood Industrial Estate, Braintree, Essex, CM7 7YN. Tel. 01376-550500.

### MIRRORS

**Lance Roberts Period Mirrors**, Unit 12, Hockley Industrial Centre, Hooley Lane, Redhill, Surrey, RH1 6JF. Tel. 01737-767430.

**The Looking Glass of Bath**, 96 Walcot Street, Bath, Avon, BA1 5BG. Tel. 01225-461969. Specialist traditional mirrors or special styles made to order.

**Overmantles of Battersea**, 66 Battersea Bridge Road, London, SWII 3AG. Tel. 0171-223 8151. Large traditional-style mirrors.

## MOSAICS AND MURALS

**Mosaicus**, 25 Salisbury Road, Hove, E. Sussex, BN3 3AE. Tel. 01273-729291. Friezes, floors and furniture in ceramic and glass mosaic.

**Murals by Lesley Saddington**, 43b Shakespeare Road, London, SE24 OLA. Tel. 0171-733 0527 or 0171-926 4855.

**Simon Fiddlehead Murals**. Tel. 0161-860 7602 or 0181-989 9324 for pamphlet and details.

**Stoneworks**, PO Box 198, Chesterfield, Derbyshire, S40 IFQ. Tel. 01246-550600. Original mosaic designs.

**White Whale Mosaics**. Tel. 01202-476685. Picture and decorative panels.

## ORGANIZATIONS

**British Bathroom Council**, Federation House, Station Road, Stoke on Trent, Staffs, ST4 2RT. Tel. 01782-747074. Fax 01782-747161.

**Disability Information Trust**, Mary Marlborough Centre, Nuffield Orthopaedic Centre, Headington, Oxford, OX3 7LD. Tel. 01865-227592.

**Disabled Living Foundation**, 380–384 Harrow Road, London, W9 2HU. Tel. 0171-289 6111.

**Institute of Plumbing**, 64 Station Lane, Hornchurch, Essex, RM12 6NB. Tel. 01708-472791. Fax 01708-448987.

## RADIATORS

**Bisque**, Head Office and details of local stockists: 15 Kingsmead Square, Bath, Avon, BA1 2AB. Tel. 01225-469244. Showroom: 244 Belsize Road, London, NW6 4BT. Tel. 0171-328 2225.

**Stiffkey Bathrooms**, Stiffkey, Wells-Next-the-Sea, Norfolk, NR23 1AJ. Tel. 01328-830 084. Reconditioned and salvaged radiators.

## SHELLS

**The Eaton Shell Shop**, 30 Neal Street, London, WC2H 9PS. Tel. 0171-379 6254. Shells, raffia mats, coral and other watery artefacts.

**Shell World**, 41 King's Road, Brighton, E.Sussex, BN1 1NA. Tel. 01273-327664. A selection of shells and marine accessories.

## SHUTTERS & BLINDS

**American Shutters**, 72 Station Road, London, SW13 OLS. Tel. 0181-876 5905.

**Calico Curtains**. Tel. 01372-723846 for brochure. Basic plain and coloured calico blinds and curtains from £60 by mail.

**The Final Curtain Company**, 9 Netherby Road, London, SE23. Tel. 0181-699 3826. Natural fabrics made into blinds and curtains; will make in your own fabric as well.

**Luxaflex**. For nearest stockist tel. 01698-881281 Wide range of roller and slat blinds in contemporary and traditional designs.

**Plantation Shutters**, 14 Marcus Terrace, London, SW18 2JW. For further details and brochure tel. 0181-870 7996. Fax 0181-871 0041.

**Portobello Curtain Shop**, 281 Portobello Road, London, W10. Tel. 0181-964 5763. Made-to-measure curtains and blinds. Pole- and track-fitting service available.

**Ruffle & Hook**, Florence Works, 34$^1/_2$ Florence Street, London, N1. Tel. 0171-226 0370. Curtains made to order; simple styles, hessian and jute available.

**The Shutter Shop**, Queensbury House, Dilly Lane, Hartley Wintney, Hants, RG27 8EQ. Tel. 01252-844575. Fax 01252-844718.

## TILES for both walls and floors
ADVICE

**British Ceramic Research Ltd**, Queens Road, Penkhull, Stoke on Trent, Staffs, ST4 7LQ. Tel. 01782-45431. Fax 01782-412331.

**British Ceramic Tile Council**, Federation House, Station Road, Stoke on Trent, Staffs, ST4 2RT. Tel. 01782-747147. Fax 01782-747161.

STOCKISTS

**Ceramica Blue**, 10 Blenheim Crescent, London, W11 1NN. Tel. 0171-727 0288.

**Color 1 Ceramics**, 412 Richmond Road, East Twickenham, Middx, TW1 2EB. Tel. 0181-891 0691.

**Criterion Tiles**, 196 Wandsworth Bridge Road, London, SW6 2UF. Tel. 0171-736 9610.

**Elon**, 60 Fulham Road, South Kensington, London, SW3 6HH. Tel. 0171-584 8966.

**Fired Earth**, Twyford Mill, Oxford Road, Adderbury, Oxfordshire, OX17 3HP. Tel. 01295-812088. Fax 01295-810832.

**Marlborough Tiles**, (Dept HM3D), Elcot Lane, Marlborough, Wilts, SN8 2AY.

**Paris Ceramics**, 583 King's Road, London, SW3 5UH. Tel. 0181-675 2255 for further stockists.

**The Tile Gallery**, 1 Royal Parade, 247 Dawes Road, Fulham, London, SW6 7RE. Tel. 0171-385 8818.

**World's End Tiles**, British Rail Yard, Silverthorne Road, London, SW8 3HE. Tel. 0171-720 8358.

## UNITS

**Hayloft Woodwork**, 3 Bond Street, Chiswick, London, W4 1QZ. Tel. 0181-747 3510.

**John Lewis of Hungerford**, Park Street, Hungerford, Berks, RG17 0EA. Tel. 01488-682 066.

**Mark Wilkinson**, Overton House, High Street, Bromham, Nr Chippenham, Wilts, SN15 2HA. Showrooms also at 126 Holland Park Avenue, London, W11 4JA. Tel. 0171-727 5814; 41 St John's Wood High Street, London, NW8 7NJ. Tel. 0171-586 9579; 13 Holywell Hill, St Albans, Herts, AL1 1EZ. Tel. 01727-840 975; 4 High Street, Maidenhead, Berks, SL6 1QJ. Tel. 01628-777622; 17 King Street, Knutsford, Cheshire, WA16 6DW. Tel. 01565-650800.

**Rhode Design**, 65 Cross Street, London, N1 2BB. Tel. 0171-354 9933.

**Smallbone of Devizes**, 105–109 Fulham Road, London SW3 6RL. Tel. 0171-581 9989. Other showrooms in Knutsford, Devizes, Harrogate, Leamington Spa, Tunbridge Wells.

## Acknowledgements

The publisher should like to thank the following sources for providing the photographs for this book:

**Robert Harding Picture Library/IPC Magazines** 14, 15 left and right, 16 bottom, 28 right, 29 bottom right, 31 top left and right, 32 bottom, 38 top, centre and bottom, 41 bottom, 70, /**Jan Baldwin** 6 bottom left, 28 top left, 29 left of centre, 33 top, 35 bottom, 37 right, 76 top left, 82 bottom, 85 top, /**David Barrett** 44 right, 47 right, /**Tim Beddow** 48, 52 top left, 64 top, 79 left of centre, 87 top, /**Simon Brown** 27 top left, 32 top, /**Henry Bourne** 11 top left, 19 left, /**Linda Burgess** 77 bottom right, 82 top, /**Christopher Drake** 8 bottom left, 18 bottom, 26 top left and bottom left, 27 bottom right, 30, 31 bottom, 36 top, 39 top and bottom, 64 bottom, 77 top left, 78 bottom left, 80, 81, 87 bottom, /**Brian Harrison** 58 right, 59, /**Hugh Johnson** 78 right, 83 bottom, /**Ken Kirkwood** 7 bottom right, 79 top left, 85 bottom, /**Les Meehan** 77 left of centre, /**James Merrell** 9, 26 right, 29 top, 33 bottom, 42 top left, 45 left of centre, 46 top and bottom, 47 top left and bottom, 65, 88, /**David Parmitter** 84, /**Jonathan Pilkington** 63, /**Trevor Richards** 6 right, 10 bottom left and right, 17 left and right, 34, 53 left of centre, 66, 69, 76 bottom left, 78 top left, 83 top, 86, 91, /**Peter Rauter** 41 top, /**Debbie Treloar** 8 top left, 12 top left, 44 bottom left, 44 bottom right, /**Andreas von Einsiedel** 35 top, 36 bottom, 55 bottom right, 71 bottom, /**Fritz von der Schulenburg** 71 top, /**Polly Wreford** 37 left.

The author would like to acknowledge **The House Plant Expert** by Dr D. G. Hessayan.

**Ken Kirkwood** 16 bottom
**Andreas von Einsiedel** 13 bottom right, 21 right, 79 bottom right, 90.